THE OTHER WORLD

BY NATALIA LUCIA AGUILAR GAONA

This story was first published in Spanish under
the name "El Otro Mundo" and was distributed
by DEMAC A.C. In 2001 as part of short stories anthology.

The English translation from the original Spanish version was
written by
Natalia Lucia Aguilar Gaona
as well as the design, cover art work and all illustrations
January 2011

Publishing

All copy rights reserved by the author.

Special thanks to Allan H. Cutler JD. PhD for
his encouragement and proofreading.

CONTENTS

Chapter I
    PAST CONSTELLATIONS   1

Chapter II
    FALLING FROM GRACE   7

Chapter III
    LAND OF LEGENDS   13

Chapter IV
    THE INVISIBLE WORLD   21

Chapter V
    ARROWS   33

Chapter VI
    ABDUCTED   41

Chapter VII
    DWELLERS OF REDEMPTION   53

Index   59

TO ALL MY BELOVED,
SPECIALLY
JUAN AND JULIAN

Chapter 1

PAST CONSTELLATIONS

It was Saturday morning in Mexico City, on February tenth 2001; I had forty minutes left, before boarding the ten-thirty bus at the East terminal station. After purchasing my ticket to Calpulalpan, one of the largest municipalities in the state of Tlaxcala. Piles of materials lay everywhere, I sat quietly with my briefcase on a few cement bricks in a rather secluded area, partly closed off to the public due to the remodeling of the bus station's new cafeteria. I was completely relaxed and felt a bit drowsy, when a loud snapping noise violently woke me up; the sharp blow of discarded material carelessly tossed into a metal container instantly took me back to the most tragic and horrible event in my life, the moment I lost my innocence.

Here on this planet, some people get to live a complacent and rather comfortable life, free of inconveniences but monotonous. Ha but, the "Wretched people" are not those lost souls wrapped in newspapers sleeping on the sidewalks. No, they are a breed of useless beings indistinguishable to the eye, thriving at the expense of others. These hubris and insensitive parasites lead a meaningless existence and their legacy is evident, leaving everywhere deep irreversible scars and devastation. Nevertheless, there is another kind of being. We are a hybrid of persons known as "the inspired" prone to create harmony, with a hypersensitive conscience and physiology.

I believe that throughout our young existence and of course according to our own particular culture, we are handed down a cluster of shiny beliefs, all well intended and the sum of a collective effort to make sense of things around us. Some spiritual concepts are meant to help us accept the magnitude of destructive forces of natural phenomenon. Yet first, to enter that spiritual realm one must possess the capability to perceive all those forces...

Growing up in a bi-cultural home meant assimilating two different sets of values. My parents kept me swinging in a morbid mix of incoherent habits and expectations which had a polarizing effect. I found myself crisscrossing between cultures. This contrast blurred any understanding. Firmly entwined with each other stood the relics of my ancestral pre-Columbian origins, prejudiced and full of remorse, juxtaposed to Anglo-American idealism; exploitative, indifferent and unscrupulous.

My self-denying mother lived in a universe totally dependent on God's divine good will. This also meant she was free to interpret the Holy Scriptures to her own convenience, by believing "Help thy self, because God is busy ". Just as many devoted Catholic women of the 60's she was abandoned by the aloofness of her own faith, turning her loyalty to the only deity and master of our time, the unquestionable money Lord. She bought everything she desired, but in exchange she lost what she had: her life.

Children should try to understand their parents, not judge them. If we are indeed fortunate, they may turn out to be a good example, towards the end of their dreaded elderly years. We might witness how they rejoice a life full of satisfactions, but it's a sore sight when elders parade their misfortune, an endless stream of blame, drenched in agony and lament.

My father's world was like that of most atheist men of that time; a dutiful intellectual restricted by his ideals. This led to a life of isolation and confinement. Though, he wasn't always a hermit, as a child, he was raised by his strict grandparents properly indoctrinated into the Roman Catholic religion. As a mindful alter boy he took center stage for all to see his divine devotion. The people that knew him then, could have never imagined that later in life he'd fervently condemn his Christian beliefs.

As a child my mother taught me to cherish religious art portraying adorable little angels. That joy was tarnished forever, after witnessing my father tear up my mother's favorite angel prints. Many years later I wondered whether his overwhelming need for attention might have made him jealous of her religious devotion. His rigid fantasy world was not a place where my mother could inhabit. He secretly yearned for a female android, an appliance that could be conveniently switched on or off.

Both worlds were rapidly disintegrating in a nearby constellation popularly known as North America, the dream factory. The dream being highly volatile and always imposing to those wide eyed couples fleeing Mexico from its impoverished legacy. My parents innocently choose to migrate north to rid themselves of a generation of civil war survivors paralyzed by fear. Disillusioned and frustrated along with all the other uprooted immigrants seeking to purchase a dream, it sadly became an unattainable fantasy.

Each of us have many choices but only one life. Sometimes options are scarce. It's easy to be dazzled by the classy looks of a world with apparent comforts and functionality. I can't blame my parents for trying their best. Towards the end of the nineteen fifties, striving for that particular brand of excellence made a great deal of sense. But, for those from a lower class there were no choices. To explain this contradiction, I try to understand how and where it all began. It seemed irresistible for that lonesome society to be stubbornly hooked on or addicted to "the illusion of success" or better yet "the best choice".

The Other World
by Natalia Lucia Aguilar Gaona

Chapter 11

FALLING FROM GRACE

Coyoacán is geographically situated in the center of the Anahuac valley. This vestige of the colonial era has survived the pressures of Mexico's mega metropolis. By 1974 late in November a couple of months had passed since I arrived. After living seventeen years in a Los Angeles suburb, I had grown tired of that hypocritical existence, saturated with drugs, greed, casual sex and indifference. It took me many years before I discovered that "Your denial is your doom" and that in fact the rest of the planet could learn quite a lot about hypocrisy from Mexico. However, at that moment, I felt totally free in this inverted world where Hernan Cortez the conquistador made his home. The nostalgic cobble stone streets gave off an unwary scent of avant-garde that danced in the air under the rays of the pounding sun.

Alienated by years of racism, my father and I decided to return to our country. We gathered the courage to nourish our poverty stricken land with what we thought was modern technology and experience. Solving Mexico's problems might have been a suitable topic for an after dinner discussion, but most intellectuals didn't have any real intentions of changing anything, nor did anyone really know how to go about it. Crushed by the weight of this brutal reality, I began living in an upside down world partly because my older sister Victoria came to live with us after three years of absence. Her presence was a crucial addition to our tiny family. She felt ashamed for flunking two years in high school. That made me end up a year above her at the Juarez Institute and due to the fact that I was much taller than Victoria, I was perceived as the eldest. Plus it was much easier to deceive everyone than to explain. I wanted to make her happy, so we lied about her age.

She had been living a few years in Mexico city guarded and adored by aunts, uncles and overprotected by our maternal grandmother. We needed each other very much, not just to share the house hold chores, but to confront different challenges. Victoria was madly in love with a guy named Luis. Our father had prohibited that relationship. Despite his threats, Victoria secretly continued seeing Luis and I was her only ally. While she enjoyed a sheltered family life, I was abandoned in the suburbs of Southern California. Attending high school, cooking for my father and taking care of household duties. My life was brimming with untold adventures, multicultural social encounters, one rape attempted by my boyfriend's brother Rupert. I concealed the incident and never mentioned a word to anyone. Wrapped in layers of secrecy towards the end of my stay, I had a brief romance with a Chilean sailor who taught me how to dance tango. There docked in San Pedro California, I witnessed a generous cargo of domestic appliances and luxury cars that were loaded into three

Chilean navy vassals, General Pinochet's "pay off" for the assassination of Allende.

By the time my puberty set in I had spent most of my time avidly watching movies on TV from distant counties and drawing or painting a kaleidoscope of morbid characters. Isolated in a one-dimensional world, I was completely forsaken; I had no one to confide in. At times, I began to feel envy of church goers because they had God on their side. All I had was my strung out imagination, I didn't even have a guardian Angel to look after me. Dreams, visions and nightmares were my private consolation. Perhaps that's why I was fascinated by my sister who was like a character from a romantic movie.

Victoria had a wide smile complemented by violet colored eyes and was always on her toes, prancing and dancing about. She shivered with excitement, jumping up every time the phone rang, expecting a call from her beloved Luis who checked in at least three times a day. He worked for the Social Health office as an assistant to the purchaser coordinator, rushing orders for the hospital's medical supplies. Appearing busy he could slip in three or four calls to Victoria. My sister felt adored by Luis but was fearful of our father's fury. She had not forgotten the reason behind our parent's torturous divorce. The physical and verbal abuse was never discussed between us. As she approached her eighteenth birthday, I knew she could never take the humiliation of a beating. Ah, but her insatiable love for Luis had turned into a blind obsession, worth risking everything…

The Other World
by Natalia Lucia Aguilar Gaona

Chapter III

LAND OF LEGENDS

Attending the Mexican education system was like jumping off a cliff and watching myself splash in all directions as I hit the flabby surface of mediocrity. It was an academic system set within a surreal legacy that was prompted by a predominantly Catholic society. To my amazement they openly disdained all of those who dared to be human. The Juarez Institute was a middle class private school; I discovered that habitual sexual harassment was a teacher's second nature and that students could effortlessly pass into the next grade with a bottle of whiskey. Feudal professors arbitrarily dominated the rowdy students with all kinds of random abuse and disrespect. Corrupt duplicity summed up a chummy relationship considered unusually amiable to all. In retaliation one student had the audacity of hiring a pair of actors to impersonate his parents, each month they'd come in and sign his report card in front of the director's assistant (better known to us as Kermit the frog) without ever getting caught. In the midst of this compulsive misbehavior and wacky name calling most of these students had something in common: they had been expelled from other schools. In academic circles the Juarez Institute was considered a dump, one of those places where parents could keep their bratty kids until finished with their middle education.

Mingling around a rowdy bunch was far from being a misfortune. These radical elements gave way to a very interesting brew, distilling a crude form of freedom for very exclusive social club. That display of rebellion was the authentic expression of our true and pure feelings, the basis for a marvelous friendship that has survived and blossomed well over twenty five years.

It was more of a state of grace that was not bestowed to just anyone. Only those forsaken could take part after, of course, going through the obligatory baptism to gain admission be christened with nicknames like: Grandpa, Broomstick, Skullface, Vallardo, Fanta, Lucas, el Tijón, la Pastora, el Panchorro, Raidela, Crocodile, el Pipucho, Catasha, Dog and Mop head.

Unwary victims fell into our indestructible web made of an alloy of comical and versatile intentions, all fabulously irreverent. A fine spectacle of arrogant teachers, neurotic nerds and silly do-gooders were lost in a useless struggle to elude our net of candid and aggressive verbal gibberish.

All Mr. Vallardo had to do was to pronounce the magical words: "Hail Chumino the Devil's pet" and immediately a sweet do-gooder transformed into a vicious mouth foaming monster, sending the entire class running terrified, out into the street stumbling and screaming.

Character is a virtue built by forces meant to sustain our personal dignity. By the end of my high school senior year I had acquired an incisive vocabulary and absurd amount of self-confidence. My oratorical abilities were often solicited by fellow students being harassed by local thugs. Immediately the word would get out, "Lucia is zooming in" surrounded by admirers, I struck directly at their egos, demolishing the scoundrels and attaining an instant victory (mustn't forget attack is the best defense). They had no idea of what hit them, completely disarmed and emotionally stripped, the paralyzed thugs stood with their jaws hanging speechless. In this cozy world the once shy and quiet teenager (me) became a fierce defender, capable of empowering others against injustice. From then on, with the wrath of one look, my colleagues could keep their furious aggressors restrained. Undoubtedly the key for survival is genuine accountability. One must earn respect from others you start by respecting thyself.

At the Institute there were two very unbelievable characters. One of the most memorable people I have ever had the pleasure of meeting was Miss Juanita, a petite woman less than four feet tall. To me she was the Juarez Institute's star and "Prima Donna". Miss Juanita's presence commanded absolute respect, teaching or should I say riding any subject like an apocalyptic jockey. She taught me not only how to appreciate literature, but also the importance of expressing the truth, a crucial component that has propelled me throughout my life. Miss Juanita possessed an innate ability to pick out the student who didn't have their homework done. As the shameless student stood there making all sorts of excuses and arguments, she would patiently listen; and with that same kind of voice in which she had asked for his homework in she'd say "You're an idiot, my dearest son, please sit down,".

The other unearthly character at the Juarez was the anatomy professor and if it wasn't for the morbidity of a certain assignment, he too would be easily forgotten. Dr. Garcia from the state of Tabasco never made eye contact. His chubby body held his sweaty head at an angle that fixed his gaze towards the ceiling. When he'd speak to a student, someone by sheer chance always asked bewildered if Dr. Garcia meant him. On a certain occasion Dr. Garcia decided that in order to learn about human bone structure, we need a skeleton, but the institute didn't own one. So, he casually came up with a skeleton contest. Coincidentally one of the alumni's father was director of cemeteries for the city. We ended up going in groups of five students to the cemetery where we had to pick up a sack of human remains for the contest. Getting to the cemetery and talking to the gravedigger was just the beginning of this repulsive assignment. All of us became seriously sick after looking inside the sack. No one told us that human remains meant the whole human body, skin, hair, muscles and ligaments. There was no way out of the ill-fated assignment. Yet since we all wanted to graduate someday, I volunteered to clean the bones and the rest of the group agreed to paint and mount the skeleton. That weekend out on the balcony at the corner of Corina and London Streets, adjacent to my apartment's living room where we lived, I placed the bones in two buckets of sodium hydroxide to soak. After rinsing them off and letting them dry out, with a metal fiber I scraped off the bits of flesh still clinging to the bone. I pondered about the fragility of our human condition and asked myself what kind of life this man or woman had? I thanked him or her for letting me wash him or her while placing the bones in another bucket with chlorine. Until then, I was unaware of the subtle capacity of molecules to transform. By grasping that reality, these ossified sculptures went beyond the spiritual world. The following Thursday, I invited the group to pick up the bleached bones that were ready for painting and mounting. Our skeleton won first place. The other groups were disqualified for purchasing their entry. Leaving only two contestants that actually used human remains.

The Other World
by Natalia Lucia Aguilar Gaona

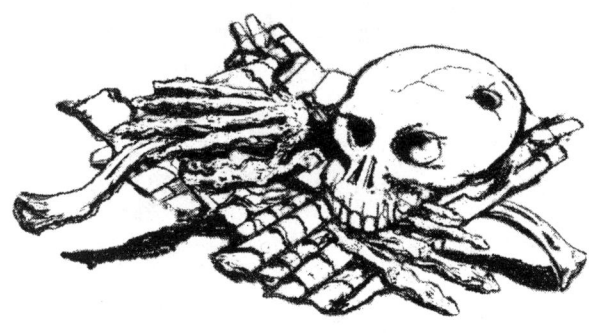

Chapter IV

THE INVISIBLE WORLD

No one knows what the future holds for us. Yet, Victoria frequently consulted a Turkish coffee reader. One day she dragged me off to see her fortune teller. To my surprise the fortune teller said that I was gifted and that I should go and work for him as a "fortuneteller" at his prestigious establishment. My devoted sister seriously believed everything he said. I suspected he wanted to have me there as a consort. He wasn't my type so I never went back.

Victoria found an article in a fashion magazine on how to read the past, present and future events with a Spanish deck of cards. She insisted I should follow the instructions for her sake and was satisfied with my first reading, so she recommended me to her friends at school. Because I neglected to charge a cent, I instantly became popular. Plus I found it amusing and just did it for fun.

Back at home we were considered slaves. My sister and I had neither rights, nor access to money. Our father a "Pure Cynic" had his own brand of twisted beliefs. On one occasion I caught my father reprimanding my bedroom door, well not exactly my door; the scolding was directed at me because he thought I was still inside my room. However I was watching his violent hollering from inside the kitchen undetected and to my surprise when he finished his furious rant, he turned around and started chuckling. He was so pleased with himself that he couldn't contain his laughter, placing his hand over his mouth, afraid I might hear him. I then stepped out of the kitchen, for him to be aware of my presence. He swiftly ran into his room slamming the door behind him pretending nothing had happened.

The Other World
by Natalia Lucia Aguilar Gaona

It was well understood that our father couldn't care less about our needs or have any sympathy for our feelings. We resorted to another solution to finance our necessities. Victoria naturally became my manager, negotiating a small fee or donation, two or three pesos after a card reading with our regular clients. Cheerfully we'd go across to "El Jarocho" a coffee shop on the corner of Allende and Moctezuma Street. There, we treated ourselves to a doughnut and a cup of coffee during our high school recess.

A guy from the senior year caught my attention at the institute. He wore his hair long and a goatee, which gave him a "Che Guevara look". As soon as I confessed my inclination, Victoria arranged a meeting with Javier, who also had taken notice of me. Thereafter we started meeting briefly after school, for no more than a few minutes. Victoria wanted us to go on a picnic. She wanted Javier to get us both out of the house to later meet somewhere with Luis. We planned everything in advance to convince our father. We said the picnic was a school group event and he gave us his permission to go. So we suggested he take his girlfriend Margaret out for lunch. We saved up some of the money we had made during the week and bought bread, ham, cheese, paper plates and cups. I was very excited. This was my first real date with Javier. He didn't have a car, so we had to use public transportation that day. The guys payed our way and bought a bottle of red wine.

None of us had ever been to "Los Dinamos forest park" although it was well within the city limits. Luis waited for us in San Angel, at the terminal where each hour a bus left to "Los Dinamos Park" and Contreras a small town near the park.

Right before my eyes, blushing uncontrollably, Victoria transformed into an elastic rose and strapped herself like a bracelet to Luis's arm. Javier took the wine that Luis bought while I was left holding the picnic basket. We happily boarded a rundown bus that didn't leave every hour. We were instructed to wait for the bus to fill up. The seats were so shabby, that the old vinyl looked more like Hawaiian hula skirts and the metal floor of the bus was so worn out that you could see the pavement through it. None of those things mattered. We sat down and bought some lemon popsicles from a passing vendor while hikers, women with children, men in hats, bundles and groceries made their way onto the ancient vehicle. Burdened with a heavy foreign accent, I felt ashamed of my inability to speak Spanish fluently. Javier gladly gave me extended answers to my brief questions.

The journey up the mountain road took over two hours due to the numerous bus stops along the way. As I gazed at the lush vegetation for the first time in years, this little outing gave me the opportunity to understand the proximity of a dense forest, practically hugging the city. I was immersed in a green world. Here and there a red rug of dry pine needles covered the few, barely visible homes. Out of the ledges growing between the tiles on the rooftops, plants and trees were sprouting. Compared to where I grew up in the arid Californian desert and its scarce vegetation, my eyes began drinking in the landscape like a thirsty Bedouin approaching an oasis. Awaiting our arrival was a harmonious realm of tranquility. Stretching our numb legs, we were eager to hike the mountain. Searching for the perfect place for our first picnic, we went off the main path and into the forest, circling the mountain. To my amazement I quickly ran out of breath. I had no idea the altitude could have such a strange affect on me. Raised at sea level in Southern California, life was certainly beautiful.

Victoria started remembering our life by the ocean, full of sandcastle days at the beach. We shared nostalgic memories of a distant world. A common place lost in time for a Mexican family living in exile.

There was the perfect picnic spot! Overlooking Mexico's majestic valley, under a blue sky wiped clean by the South Pacific winds, we could see clearly to the northern mountain range, across the entire valley of Anahuac. Shining like jewels almost within reach, the snow covered volcanoes seemed like a colossal crown. We where sitting high up on the far side of a not so obvious crater.

The Other World
by Natalia Lucia Aguilar Gaona

Extending an old blanket on the slope we felt extremely exhausted and hungry, ready to feast on our humble lunch. Although it was mid November a semitropical climate prevailed, the strong pine scent mixed with the wine's weak aroma filling the air as we shared our plans for the future; the way's we each viewed it, Javier applied at the Polytechnical National Institute. Luis was also finishing high school and had no idea what to study. Victoria pictured herself as a English teacher and I was thinking of Fine Arts, as a carrier option though intrigued by my vocational test that suggested mechanical engineering.

Being ashamed of sounding foolish made me an avid listener. At school, making fun of me was kind of a sport, sometimes a real riot. The students in my classroom cracked up at my many failed attempts to pronounce words rooted in Nahuatl. I'd end up laughing too, watching them almost pee in their pants. Knowing how mortified I was to speak, my sister helped me out that day by changing the subject.

"Lucia is a good fortune teller and she can see the future", Victoria exclaimed with enthusiasm. "Everything she's told me has come true. She read the cards to Martha and Lourdes too", Victoria added.

"The first time I saw you, you were reading the cards to the etymology professor. What did you say to her? ", Javier asked smiling at me.

I looked up at him and answered "She is going to have a baby boy". I replied briefly

"That's it?", asked Luis.

"I don't remember anything else. It's really none of my business either", I remarked sharply.

"Is the future any of your business? If I could know which lottery number was going to win, I'd buy it and become a millionaire", Luis said.

"Very interesting, a millionaire. Is that what you want to be? ", I inquired .

"Yes, that's exactly what I want to be!", he answered laughing.

"Is your life going to be about money?", I insisted. "Something I learned from cleaning those bones for the contest, is that we don't get to keep anything… it all stays behind, even our bones", I added in a confident tone.

By defying Luis's disbelief, I gave Javier a glimpse of my dark side. Yet, Luis couldn't resist the opportunity to annoy me.

"Oh so you're saying that you really learned something at that pathetic little school", Luis said. (He was enrolled in a public school with socialist ideals, along with another seven thousand students).

Victoria intervened "Luis! Lucia has a right to her opinion. You must understand she just arrived here and has helped us get our father's permission for this picnic!", Victoria exclaimed, while standing up. "So we better enjoy it" she remarked while extending her hand out to Luis; and she lead him away to another place in the woods where they could be alone.

Javier seemed to understand how disappointing my sister's insensitive boyfriend made me feel. Luis couldn't remotely perceive life the way I did.

"Going back to our initial conversation, I want to be an architect", Javier said proudly.

"I'd like to make things better. I saw the anatomy exhibit and your drawings were certainly the best ones there. That eye section and its muscles had nice shadows", he exclaimed. "I take private painting lessons, but I only paint flowers. I'd like you to see them", Javier added sounding a bit conceded.

"Oh so you like details? ", I asked him as I started to put the used paper plates and cups back into the basket.

"Yes, I like them very much", he said.

Talking about myself made me uncomfortable whether it was about my psychic powers or my painting. For a long time I thought this ability was something that didn't have a profound effect on people, but the awesome power of suggestion is immeasurable. Over the decades I made many attempts to untangle this phenomenon, researching cognitive theories, reviewing the work of serious physiologist and their conclusions about mediums, shamans and witchcraft. I was certain that most were charlatans and con-artists. Then I discovered the importance of "Perception" and how people interpret each thing, later turning into "Belief". Humans have an enormous capacity for imagination. They can makeup hidden meanings for any kind of shape or scribble. Meaningless words take on a whole life of their own. Throughout many years of observation, I encountered women and men with extraordinary abilities and bulky bank accounts, largely fed by an elite group of devoted paranormal followers, all immensely wealthy. Like waving a magic wand, the possibility of an alternative future was achieved by simply suggesting it. Now I found that very disturbing. How can a bit of pseudo wisdom from a person who genuinely knew nothing turn a healthy person into a willful slave. I became unbearably distressed and intrigued because that person was me. There was a time when my own mother refused to speak to me because she thought I was possessed by the devil. An idea planted in my mother's head by Victoria who, in her attempt to defend me, argued that all my predictions came to fruition at the precise moment I had said. Many years later, I found out my relatives had labeled me a witch, thanks to her stories. A woman's fear of God won out over her own motherly love. I was deeply bewildered, yet a convicted prisoner to my father and an orphan to my mother. But the mystery finally unraveled. Seventeen years later I was commissioned to work at a hormonal chemical laboratory where I found the answers to all my questions: the reasons behind my abilities are in fact quite simple. We're all completely connected, human physiology is considerably noble. Life is sustained by harmonically devised mechanisms that combine many chemical elements to generate and convey electric energy. We and all other living organisms are just a dynamic manifestation of that very same energy and that's the reason why we're all connected.

Guarded by a natural bashfulness Javier and I rested on the blanket opposite each other, respectful of the conservative rules instigated by our middle class breeding. We spent what seemed to be a long time just talking about things at school, wondering why Juanita taught literature and how much I truly appreciated her style of reconstructing the many characters in the novels, always helping us read between the lines. Javier thought she was a bit incoherent. Although I sensed a bit of apprehension in about demystifying her. But to a certain degree he did respect her. Finally there was someone who could see beyond my flaws and somehow my terrible accent ceased to be a source of torment.

Chapter V

ARROWS

The sun was setting behind the mountain by the time Luis and Victoria came trotting down the mountainside. I folded the tablecloth and we made our way down to the main trail. When we reached the bus stop there was no one there. A small sign stated that the last bus left the park at five o'clock, but it was almost six. Realizing our predicament, we headed down the empty road. Javier took my hand for the first time as a gesture of reassurance. I wanted to continue our conversation, but I felt inhibited by Luis's presence.

Dusk set in with a brisk drop of temperature, but skipping down the road kept us warm. Embracing their forbidden love once again Victoria eagerly strapped herself to Luis for at least two more hours, the time estimated to reach the nearest town. The narrow winding road disappeared under the shadows of a thick forest while our figures were splattered with pale blue light from a gleaming October moon that looked more like a huge platter as the sounds of crickets saturated the atmosphere.

Javier wasn't one of the rejects from another high school. He enrolled at the Juarez because he lived five blocks away from the institute. I too was there due to the proximity of my home and to facilitate the US school validation procedures. We seemed very attracted to each other... and felt great respect for each other as well. My heart was full of love; I couldn't have imagined anything like it. Somehow I felt rewarded after all the grief inflicted by my peers. Life bestowed a vast amount of beauty and harmony just for the two of us to share.

I had no idea how different I was, nor could I see what others saw. They had always lived in this place. They had always had big families, cousins, aunts, friends, their culture, their dogmas, their fears, old scars. A quiet sorrow filled their eyes, always gazing towards the north, with an eternal mourning, hosted by hostile apathy, draped with a celestial resignation and at the same time they innocently cultivated mountains of hope and affection.

The Other World
by Natalia Lucia Aguilar Gaona

Nothing could prepare us for the future, not a world full of educators, nor the best economists. Not even the petulant technocrats could say which is "The best" way to act. And the only reason they can't foresee any disasters is because they generally overlook human stupidity while scholars are unable to define this crucial factor due to their own misconceptions. And most religious believers think "fear" is fueled by the devil, urging people to deny their own stupidity. Within every culture the power of fear has played a brutal role. Without a doubt fear alone has crushed our harmonious aspirations, instigated or repressed us throughout history. Our unpredictable reaction to fear is obviously underestimated and an excuse for destruction, sentencing our civilization to oblivion. Human stupidity is real. It's our interpretation of fear that hinders our behavior. On the other hand there are those who can see the real purpose of fear. They are known as oracles or shamans, but some cold readers use fear as a tool. But for those who really understand fear and know its a warning, a sharp arrow pointing at the source of danger, this awareness is an agonizing responsibility bestowed upon authentic clairvoyants or prophets. Fear is a warning signal and the mightiest tool. To no avail, many horribly ignorant persons misuse the power of suggestion. Unprofessional therapists or analysts and atheists abuse subtle words like "anxiety" to distract us from the presence of fear, eliminating the warning signal from life's basic formula, stubbornly referring to it as "Stress" in the attempt to conceal the awful pain caused by being scared. Failing to produce a "Cure" or resolve anything, people continue to set up safety nets suspended by false hopes and hooked to the charity of words alone. Those indoctrinated don't even bother to ask questions because they can't understand the answers. That very same night, somewhere inside the void of our own little minds, within this senseless world we stupidly ignored all the warning signs that were already manifesting themselves...

We seemed like four carefree forest gnomes, trotting happily and romantically through that nocturnal stage. Then we heard the sound of a car engine rapidly coming towards us. It was a vehicle swerving down the road and Luis immediately decided to hitch a ride. Everyone agreed it was a good idea, except for me.

"No!", I exclaimed. I hadn't seen the car, but I felt inevitable danger approaching. The engine noise got louder, Luis and Victoria's enthusiasm was contagious and swept Javier into joining them and no one would listen to me. Flapping his arms in the middle of the road, Luis jumped to the side of the narrow ditch just in time to avoid getting hit by the rattling car, that skidded to a stop forty feet away. Two stinking drunks emerged from inside the vehicle as Luis and Victoria ran over to greet them.

One guy wobbled by the roadside to pee and another guy stood next to the car and spoke to Luis.

"What's up?", the smiling drunk asked, extending his arm with a bottle of beer in his hand. "Have a drink", The drunk added.

"No thanks, man", answered Luis politely.

The only purpose of this ride was to get home fast, or at least that's what my sister and company thought. To Victoria these guys were her saviors from our fathers fury for being late which was all she wanted to avoid. I suggested we walk and wait for another car that wasn't full of drunks.

"I am not getting in that car!", I warned them. But Victoria had other plans...

"Are you crazy?", she bickered. Suddenly assuming the authority of the eldest sister.

"Get in! Can't you see its really late our father is going to kill us! ", she yelled hysterically at me.

"Well that's not important!", I replied "We're not going to get home on time any way!", I shouted back. Trying to convince her.

I wasn't afraid of our father, I knew how to confront him. I was aware of his craftiness. His soft spot was his persistent eloquence. My leverage point was his need to rationalize everything, not to mention that I simply planned on telling the truth, "We had to walk home, because we missed the bus".

Javier intervened by trying to convince me. I pointed at the four wretched men inside the car. I begged him to look at the pitiful piece of junk in front of us, banged on all sides, a shattered windshield and missing a headlight. There was a deep rattling sound coming from under the hood and that couldn't be good. It seemed the motor was going to fall apart at anytime. I begged Victoria, but she ignored me, clinching the basket already saddled to Luis in the front seat.

"Come on, we'll get home faster", Javier said. I had to surrender and conform to the pack. I sat in the back seat on Javier's lap. As I got into the car a fierce stench of fetid sweat, cheap liquor, mixed with a repulsive odor of putrid vomit made me immediately nauseous. If my suspicion was right, the phenomenal degree of human decay guaranteed an inescapable catastrophe and you needn't be a fortuneteller to predict that.

The Other World
by Natalia Lucia Aguilar Gaona

Chapter VI

ABDUCTED

Trapped inside the guts of that wheeled roach, we were set in motion down the winding road. I tried to embrace Javier and bury my nose in his wavy hair, as an attempt to filter the foul smell. It was useless, because behind the steering wheel the intoxicated foe, took to the curbs as if we were sliding down a twisted liquorice. Tossed around inside the sinister car, I ended up being seriously sick, looking through the dirty rear window of the car. I watched the road stretch behind us remembering that somewhere on that mountain, all the words we exchanged were being left behind. I asked my self, how much stupidity can one instant hold? Where is that future we dreamt of only a few hours earlier? If we ride off one of these high cliffs, can we be rescued? Who is going to identify our mangled corpses scattered among the metal scraps? Why would anyone bother? After the gas tank explodes surely, all traces of our incipient existence would be erased. Once again we were completely forsaken...

The sharp turns and swings kept me swallowing saliva instinctively, in a effort to avoid dizziness. Having said good bye to all hope and the universe as I knew it, I felt like crying, but I couldn't even breath. My body wanted to throw up, but there wasn't much to expel. I embraced Javier in my arms as if it was the last time. I could feel his shirt damp with perspiration. I knew he was scared too, but a man's role is to be brave. He's forced to nullify any feelings. In a strange way his warm body consoled me. I wanted somehow to free him, to let him know that he was not at fault and that perhaps we weren't meant to be lovers and at this precise moment neither of us would probably ever live to know what its like to love or be loved. With each passing curve I sadly thought our tragic end was near while eluding the abyss.

Then, a faint sound of music was barely audible. Somewhere a band was playing! We both cheered up and I thought to myself we're almost there! We all were anxious to get out of that car and make it safely back to Coyoacán without a scratch. I unraveled myself letting Javier loose from the tight knot I had turned into. With a hopeful spirit renewed, we gazed tenderly at each other. I turned my head awkwardly towards the front of the vehicle trying to get a glimpse of the town. Between the pine trees, I could distinguish some distant lights of what seemed to be a fair. As we approached the town it was confirmed, the little town of Contreras was celebrating. It was bursting with people, rows of food stands and kiddie rides. I then recalled the people who rode on the bus with us that morning, the women with their braided hair and fancy jewelry holding their babies. I remembered how the men, wearing their typical hats, were talking to smiling youngsters, the beautifully embroidered cloths covering the heavy baskets and packages overflowing with food wrapped in newspaper. It was clear now, people had left the park earlier to come to the fair. That's why the park was empty. They were all here preparing the celebration. The noisy rides and shouting vendors got louder, I imagined Javier and myself happy and relieved, walking among the stands and the rides, recognizing the faces of the people from the bus.

Unfortunately for us, nothing in our wildest imagination could prepare us for what was about to take place. In the front seat of the car, Luis sat with Victoria on his lap slightly leaning against the car door, facing the driver, while Luis could see straight ahead. Each of us had a different point of view, not just because of the place we occupied in the car, but because of our ideas and inexperience. Getting out of this mobile hell was all we wanted, yet at that moment we could never know how much of an inconvenience this free ride would turn out to be.

The road became the town's main street where the celebration was in full swing. Now, the driver didn't even blink, and I call him "the driver", because I lack the imagination to describe the imbecile who never slowed down or bothered to step on the car's brake. Like a crazy bull, he attacked and shredded the innocent bystanders at the fair. A torpedo destroying everything in its path, in just a few moments he killed, mutilated and transformed the festival into an incomprehensible blood bath. Unable to bear it, I closed my eyes and sunk my head into Javier's exhausted neck. But that didn't save me from the horrible experience. No, on the contrary, those terrifying sounds were burned forever into my memory. As the tires turned I could hear whatever fell in our way: the blunt thumps of bones crushed under the car, sticks banged, pots cracked, cloth tore.

That was the moment I lost my innocence. Gone was my bubble, smashed under waves of uncertainty and swallowed by the ferocity of my own ignorance, I was forced to swim in that ghoulish gush left behind when we die... In this alternative dimension time ceased to exist. Pierced by this new reality, I was flooded with the concentrated acid of veracity that corroded every single vestige of understanding. This is when my soul awakened and all my senses were sharpened. Yes, this was another world, an infamous place of horror and devastation unjustifiable, purely illogical, but entirely human. It's hard to make any sense of this new world. When one is lost, disoriented and completely forsaken.

I can't restore my innocence, nor can I runway from the truth. The cries for help have never stopped, they just get louder.

While the furious clamors of crowds grotesquely resonated in slow motion, "Murderers! Murderers! Stop them! Murderers!"

I couldn't believe what I heard, so I straightened up my head to see just what was happening. An outraged mob shouted and cried. As we were being chased, men and women, with their faces distorted, slammed their hands against the slippery car.

There was no way to escape, totally smothered by the immensity of human stupidity. One by one each of the lives extinguished stabbed my soul. Why do I confess this after so many years? Certainly to remind us that "Your denial is your doom". Do these wounds ever heal? No, they never heal. I merely learned to live with them. The impact of this tragedy translated into a series of irreplaceable values; correcting injustice was inspired by the frustration of innocent victims. Unmasking hypocrisy emerged from substance abuse. And finally the need to pay immediate attention to our natural senses due to the crucial importance of fear, were all results of the massacre. That's why I speak up, to abolish indifference and to kill apathy.

Nobody knew how or why we escaped. Did the Holy Spirit intervene? Down the thin road the elusive vehicle continued its descent, leaving the town and the shouting mob alone to tend to their tragedy. The car seemed to fly, silently numb, unable to utter a sound, petrified or lifeless. With no sense of speed or distance, we were suspended or frozen in a timeless world for a concise eternity.

Then, I dared to break the spell.
"Can you drop us off, please?", I said, loud and firm. Unfortunately this woke up the driver from his trance like slumber and he quickly began to threaten us.

"You guys are skewered*!", said the driver with the worst of intentions. At that precise moment, I imagined our cold body's tossed in some dark forgotten place...

But then Javier wisely responded:

"Come on man, we didn't see nothing", then the two drunk guys sitting next to us, decided to help us by pointing out all the inconveniences. One sat up and leaned over to add in a rusty voice. "Don't skewer* around; how much more do you want to screw things up? We've got enough skewering* shit to deal with. They're just kids, stop being an ass", he said half asleep. But the driver kept on threatening us.

"You're so skewered*, if you people even try to mess with me!", he responded in a barking tone, while pressing his foot on the accelerator.

For all we knew this guy might be armed. After witnessing his incredible accomplishment, no one would doubt the words of this wretched man. Once again Javier bravely reaffirmed:

"Come on, no one saw a thing". Then Luis also added to his argument.

"Look man, we couldn't have seen a thing with that basket and her in the way. Really now, we didn't see a thing".

Somehow this line of reason had a positive effect on the driver because a few seconds later the driver said:

---

*"Skewered" This word replaces an expletive than cannot be reproduced here.

"Alright you guys, just cuz I am in a good mood. Otherwise, I would skewer* you and the bitches too", while violently bursting into laughter.

Roaming through the night, astray in the outskirts of the city he drove us around and around on the deserted streets. I began to think he wasn't convinced at all and maybe was looking for a quiet place to kill us. The driver looked disturbed. From my uncomfortable position, I could see his right eye gleaming between his swollen eyelids. Then he stepped on the brake, stopping for the first time since we got in.

We were practically ejected from the car, wobbling out on our legs still numb. Luis couldn't stop thanking those wicked idiots, who drove off without uttering a word. I gave Victoria a decapitating look, but I knew it wasn't her fault. It was an instinctive priority to accommodate our insensitive father, yet his uncontainable bad temper was impossible to avoid. That night I had the proof that "Your denial is your doom". Her urge to be on time, almost made us all permanently late.

Our father's bitter personality forced us to lead a double life. To survive, we had to lie to him. We had to protect him from the truth because we loved him and he was our only next of kin. He despised our presence and disapproved of everything we did. His bitter character was an excuse to bypass an unwanted obligation. The curse of a perfectionist is that they yearn for excellence and frown at mediocrity, yet end up choking uncontrollably with their own incompetence.

But feeling outraged was never going to erase these atrocities. I wanted the criminals convicted. Naturally, it was Luis who first spoke up and argued on just how stupid my logic was.

"Don't even think of accusing them!", he said brimming with anger. Victoria and Javier did their best to explain why we wouldn't gain a thing if we tried to turn in the criminals. Once again, I had to bite my tongue and admit just how naïve I was.

"When has any authority in this country ever cared about justice?", They shouted at me. This is big!

"Newspapers will lynch us. They'll make us responsible for the whole thing, because the police will never bother to catch the real culprits. They will get away with murder regardless of our innocence".

"This can't be!", I said, as my eyes burst into the tears that I could no longer contain.

"That's it, remember no one saw anything!", Luis shouted obviously agitated.

Lost who knows where, it took us another half an hour to find a street with a bit more traffic in search of a taxi that could get us home. I didn't want any pity from them so I retreated and walked alone, while thinking to myself that there will never be enough tears to bring back all those lost lives, nor could I bring forth enough good intentions to repair those maimed at the fair. Enraged with helplessness, I thought my head would explode. They looked at me with pity because I didn't want to understand or accept, that's how things are in Mexico. I had to learn fast. According to them "the truth has no purpose. You'll suffer a thousand and one disappointments if you don't learn to hold your tongue".

The Other World
by Natalia Lucia Aguilar Gaona

"Nothing will ever change" it's a life style inherited long before the conquistadors had made there way over here. "No body has the courage to be different". Why should they? Life didn't rob me of my innocence; I pushed it over a cliff. It died crushed under the wheels. The truth can't be hidden and there is no divine forgiveness for those who are different.

Chapter VII

DWELLERS OF REDEMPTION

Certainly enough, the events of that day were never mentioned again. I excused myself with Javier when he came calling. I told him that I could no longer continue to see him. I think he understood the reason why without any explanation. I never saw him again. My sister got pregnant the following year and married Luis who turned out to have the same explosive temper as our old dear dad. Victoria suffered twenty five years of physical and verbal abuse. Curiously, in spite of finishing a bachelors and masters degree, she still reads her horoscope everyday, alternating an eight hour job with three children. Luis didn't finish any of the three different careers he started. He was involved in a number of fraudulent businesses and of course Victoria bailed him out every time. She was constantly sick and survived uterus cancer, finding the strength to leave him if he didn't get help. Luis stopped drinking and goes to his AA meetings. Also he's trying to control his temper. Only a few months ago, he called me to ask for my forgiveness. Of course, I asked him not to use words but to speak with good deeds... I don't believe my sister deserves to be mistreated, nor should she give up the hope of being happy.

The voices persisted pleading for help and each day they got louder and multiplied. I aged twenty years that night and totally stopped speaking, limiting my oral expressions to a minimum. It no longer had anything to due with my accent, but because I was convinced that no one cared to hear what I wanted to say. Religion and politics were banished from my life. I went on to study architecture, but I lived off my creative abilities. Somehow I started screaming with colors, becoming a visual innovator. Directly inserted in the middle of the advertising business, precisely at the time when the power of visualization took on unprecedented dimensions, I'd say that the second half of the last century was totally saturated with images: Corporate images, soft drinks, electro-domestic brands, cosmetics, detergents, records, movies, videos, computers, and cars. Antagonistic images, like angry protesters marching, wars, famine, people wounded in disasters, earthquakes, floods, ghettos, jails, mountains of garbage and victims of AIDS. Spectacular images like that of a fetus still growing inside a womb, distant constellations, mountain ranges, the Alps, the Andes, the Himalayas, the earth seen from the moon, the Olympics and of course religious images, extraterrestrials, ghosts, fairies and angels, all these images were instantly available for mass consumption.

Though I survived a thousand and one disappointments, I could never bring myself to believe that Mexico could cradle that much hypocrisy. Not when the dwellers of this land discover little by little with each beat of their heart, the light within their soul. Those who dare to cultivate the art of living become "nahuales": like birds nesting between vertical spaces known as apartments they're virtually airborne, lightweight feathered creatures that dissolved into mid air. We can transform into modest little gofers and travel underground in trains called subways. When outside we change swiftly into lovely little mice running impeccably through a congested labyrinth of downtown city streets and at night we drink like thirsty jaguars in caves know as bars. Then like contortionist monkeys we dance at parties and night clubs and like lazy bears we want to sleep anywhere and if we could all day. One day I turned into an eagle and freed myself. I flew off taking both my sons away from the land of appearances and conditioned responses. I escaped the world of "the beautiful people". I gave up my prestigious company, I abandoned the addict and I broke my commitment to a phony marriage. I decided to stand on my own principles, those that I once hesitated to defend like an ancient song yearning to be shared. Moving beyond enlightenment, "I stopped denying" and replaced that bad habit with pure harmony! I entered the other world, one where there is no need for lies or injustice, a place where energy flows. I discovered that it doesn't matter how much we may know or have, it's all worthless if we don't share it. In this new world, I learned to trust again, to love and be loved. After all, we are not the architects of our own destiny. We are persistence cultivators, planting and growing benevolence and love-ability. There will come many harsh storms and cold seasons. Stay aware and be prepared. Take in those who are forsaken, because we shall always have our own inner light to share and keep us warm.

That banging noise took me back to that mournful moment of my past. The whole day, I relived that horrible tragedy of all those forsaken people. I was compelled to forget, but it became indispensable to recall. That very same day I returned from Tlaxcala and my affection for good coffee took me to "El Jarocho" where I met with Hector, one of the owners, and we started to talk about the days when his parents only owned that coffee shop. He was fifteen back then, but he remembered my fortune telling days. The reminiscences of a shared past gave way to a warm glow in our eyes. We evoked memories of the skeleton contest, lingering echoes of infamous nicknames, Juanita our unforgettable literature professor came to mind. Contemplating the smile of a familiar face, I paid for the coffee and thanked him for preserving this place of convergence. I returned to my sanctuary, grabbed the phone and dialed Aida's number, an old friend from the Juarez institute.

"Hi, I need to tell you something", I said before she even uttered a word. Then I added. "This is something I have never ever told anyone… "

May 23, 2001

Index

Abuse 14, 46, 53,
Abyss 43,
Academic 10, 13
Aida's 53,
Allende 10, 23,
Alps 55,
American
    Anglo 3,
    North 4,
Anahuac, of valley 7, 26,
Ancestral 3,
Andes 55,
Android 4,
Angel 4, 8,
Architects 57,
Arrow 35,
Baptism 15,
Bears 56,
Bedouin 25,
Benevolence 49,
Bi-cultural 2,
Broomstick 15,
Bus 24, 37, 46,
California
    Southern 2, 9, 25,
    San Pedro 8,
Californian 25,
Calpulalpan 1,
Catasha 15,
Catholic 4, 13,
Che Guevara 23,
Chilean 8, 9,
Christian 4,
Chumino 15,
Clairvoyants 35,

Contreras 24, 43,
Corina 18,
Cortez, Hernan 8,
Coyoacan 6, 43
Criminals 50,
Crocodile 15,
Culprits 51,
Culture 2,
Cynic 22,
Denial 8, 40, 46, 49,
Devil's 15,
Devoted 3,
Devotion 4,
Dinamos Park 24, 21,
Disillusioned 5,
Divine 4,
Dog 13,
Dogmas 34, 43,
Donna, Prima 17,
Downtown 56,
Dream 4, 5,
Dreams 8, 10,
Education 10, 14,
Eagle 56,
Electro-domestic 55,
Eternity 47,
Excellence 5, 50,
Extraterrestrials 55,
Fanta 15,
Father 8, 9, 18, 22, 38, 49,
Father's 4, 8, 45,
Festival 45,
Feudal 14,
Forces 2,
Foreign accent 21,

Forgiveness 54,
Forsaken 15, 35, 45, 42, 57,
Fortuneteller 21, 39, 50,
Friendship 11,
Functionality 5,
Future 28, 42,
Garcia, Dr. 17,
Geographically 6,
God 3, 10, 26,
Gofers 56,
Grace 6,
    State of 11,
Grandpa 12,
Grandparents 4,
Harmony 2, 34,
Hawaiian 24,
Hector 57,
Hermit 4,
High school 8,
Himalayas 55,
Holy Scriptures 4,
    Spirit 47,
Homework 17,
Human 10, 18, 39
Hypocrisy 8, 43, 46, 55,
Idealism 3,
Images 55,
Immigrants 5,
Injustice 16,
Innocence 1, 41, 45, 51, 48,
Innocent 38,
Insensitive 2,
Irresistible 5,
Jaguars 56,
Jarocho El, 23, 24, 57,
Javier 23, 24, 40, 44, 47, 49, 50, 53,
Juanita, Miss 16, 17, 57,

Juarez's 11, 17
    Juarez Institute 8, 17, 53,
Justice 50,
Kermit 14,
Kin 50,
Labyrinth 56,
Legacy 5,
London 18,
Lord 3,
Los Angeles 7,
Lourdes 27,
Lucia 16, 27,
Lucas 15,
Luis 7, 9, 23, 27, 34, 40, 44, 46, 47, 49, 50, 54,
Lynch 50,
Maimed 51,
Margaret 23,
Martha 28,
Massacre 47,
Mediocrity 10, 50,
Millionaire 28,
Mexican 13, 26,
Mexico 4, 8, 43, 45, 48, 51,
    City 1, 8,
Mexico's 6, 8, 23, 47
Mice 56,
Moctezuma 23,
Money 3, 22,
Monkeys 56,
Mop head 15,
Monster 15,
Morbid 9,
Mountain 25, 26, 35,
    range 21, 27,
Multicultural 9,
Murderers 42,

Nahuales 48,
Nahuatl 27,
Naïve 46,
Nerds 12
Newspapers 2, 50,
Noise 3, 57,
Nostalgic 6,
Obligatory 11,
Olympics 51,
Oracles 35,
Oratorical 16,
Pacific 26,
Panchorro, el 12,
Paralyzed 5,
Pastora la 13,
Perception 25,
Perfectionist 43
Physiology 26
Pipucho, el 15,
Police 46,
Politics 50,
Pregnant 53,
Prophets 35,
Public school 23,
Racism 7,
Radical elements 11,
Raidela 15,
Rape 8,
Rebellion 11,
Religion 4, 50,
Religious Art 4,
Religious images 55,
Reminiscences 53,
Rupert 9,
Sanctuary 53,

San Angel 24,
Sexual harassment 10,
Shamans 35,
Skeleton 17, 19, 57,
Skull-face 15,
Society 10,
Sodium hydroxide 18,
Soul 45, 55,
Souls 2,
Spell 47,
Spanish 21, 25,
Spiritual
    Realm 2,
    Concepts 2,
Stupidity 42, 46,
Suburb 6, 9
Tabasco 17,
Tango 9,
Taxi 51,
Technocrats 32,
Technology 7,
Thugs 16,
Tijón el 15,
Tlaxcala 1, 57,
Tongue 51,
Underground 56,
Universe 3,
Vallardo 15,
Victims 15, 46, 55,
Victoria 7, 8, 9, 23, 21, 27, 26, 34, 35, 40, 45, 46, 49, 54,
World 4, 7, 21, 45, 42, 43,
Wretched 2, 38, 48,
    People 2,

Made in the USA
San Bernardino, CA
14 November 2017